ARTIST TRANSCRIPTIONS SAXOPHONE

THE Charlie Parker COLLECTION

Transcribed by Forrest "Woody" Mankowski

Photo by William "PoPsie" Randolph
copyright 2005 Michael Randolph
www.PoPsiePhotos.com
PoPsie-Photos@att.net

ISBN 0-634-09416-5

HAL•LEONARD® CORPORATION

7777 W. BLUEMOUND RD. P.O. BOX 13819 MILWAUKEE, WI 53213

Visit Hal Leonard Online at
www.halleonard.com

Charlie Parker
BIOGRAPHY

Born in Kansas City in 1920, Charlie Parker was the only son of Charles and Addie Parker. His first contact with music came in school, where at an early age he played baritone horn in the school band. At the age of 15, Parker started showing great interest in the alto saxophone, drawn to the music he heard in alleyways coming from jam sessions in Kansas City nightspots. In 1935, he left school to completely dedicate himself to being a musician, working with several Kansas City jazz and blues bands while honing his craft. In 1938, Parker joined the band of pianist Jay McShann, touring in Chicago and New York. He made the move to live in New York in 1939, staying there for almost a year while working as a professional musician and sitting in on jam sessions. The charged musical atmosphere was starting to have an influence on Parker's playing style.

Returning to Kansas City to attend his father's funeral, Parker rejoined Jay McShann and in 1940 made his first recordings with the band. He got the chance to solo on recordings such as "Hootie Blues," "Sepian Bounce," and the 1941 hit "Confessing the Blues". While on tour with McShann in 1942, Parker sat in on jam sessions in Harlem, catching the ear of such artists as Dizzy Gillespie and Thelonious Monk. That same year he broke off from McShann and joined pianist Earl Hines for eight months, reuniting with Dizzy Gillespie. By 1944, Parker and Gillespie were part of Billy Eckstine's band, along with other up-and-coming players. Parker headlined his own band with Gillespie in 1945, taking the group to Hollywood in December of that year. These were historic performances; both the band lineup and audiences were racially diverse.

Parker continued to perform in Los Angeles until 1946, when he suffered a nervous breakdown and was confined at a state hospital, the result of heroin and alcohol addiction. After being released in 1947, Parker continued working in Los Angeles, making more records for the Dial label. In April of 1947, he came back to New York and formed a seminal quintet consisting of Miles Davis, Duke Jordan, Tommy Potter and Max Roach.

Parker became larger than life from 1947 to 1951, playing clubs, concerts, broadcast performances, and touring with Jazz at the Philharmonic. There was a controversial recording session with strings that eventually became one of the most popular recordings he ever did. During this active period in his life, Parker's dependence on drugs worsened. He began to get a reputation for being a no-show at performances, even pawning his saxophone several times to keep his habit going. It came to a head in 1951 when Parker's New York cabaret license was revoked by the city's narcotics squad. The license was reinstated two years later, but the damage had already been done. His health was declining steadily and he twice attempted suicide before committing himself to Bellevue Hospital in 1954. His last public appearance was at Birdland, the club named in his honor, in 1955. Parker died seven days later.

Charlie Parker has come to be known as one of the most influential jazz musicians in the history of the idiom. His stylistic innovations are a constant source of inspiration that continue to be passed on from musician to musician.

The Bird

from *20th Century Masters: The Millennium Collection* (Verve 29002)

By Charlie Parker

E♭ Alto Saxophone

Bird Feathers

from *The Legendary Dial Masters, Vol. I* (Stash ST-CD-23)

By Charlie Parker

Bird of Paradise

from *The Legendary Dial Masters, Vol. I* (Stash ST-CD-23)

By Charlie Parker

E♭ Alto Saxophone

Moderately ♩ = 122

Dizzy Atmosphere

from *Dizzy Gillespie-Shaw 'Nuff* (Musicraft MVSCD-53)

By John "Dizzy" Gillespie

Confirmation
from *Now's the Time* (Verve 825 671-2)
By Charlie Parker

Eb Alto Saxophone

Cool Blues

from *The Legendary Dial Masters, Vol. I* (Stash ST-CD-23)

By Charlie Parker

E♭ Alto Saxophone

Dexterity

from *The Legendary Dial Masters, Vol. I* (Stash ST-CD-23)

By Charlie Parker

E♭ Alto Saxophone

Bright Swing ♩ = 212

Embraceable You

from *The Legendary Dial Masters, Vol. I* (Stash ST-CD-23)

Music and Lyrics by George Gershwin and Ira Gershwin

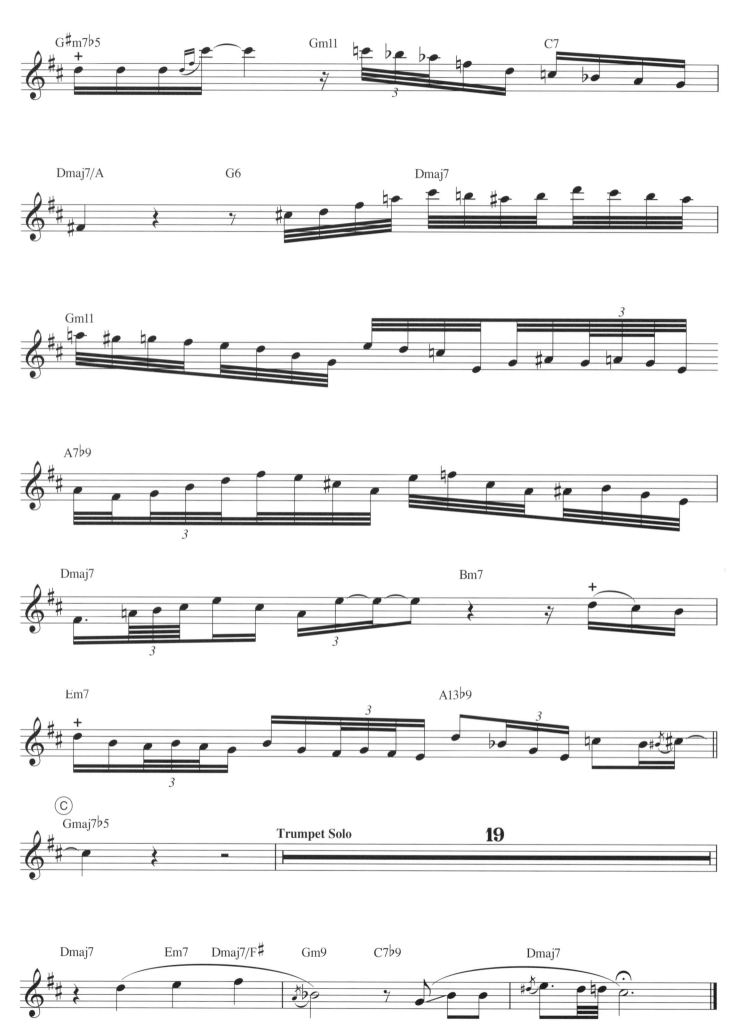

I Didn't Know What Time It Was

from *Charlie Parker with Strings, The Master Takes* (Verve 314 523 984-2)

Words by Lorenz Hart
Music by Richard Rodgers

E♭ Alto Saxophone

Groovin' High

from *Dizzy Gillespie-Shaw 'Nuff* (Musicraft MVSCD-53)

By John "Dizzy" Gillespie

E♭ Alto Saxophone

Moderate Swing ♩ = 192

I'll Remember April

from *Charlie Parker with Strings: The Master Takes* (Verve 314 523 984-2)

**Words and Music by Pat Johnson,
Don Raye and Gene De Paul**

In the Still of the Night

from *The Cole Porter Songbook* (Verve 823 250-2)

Words and Music by Cole Porter

Lover Man

(Oh, Where Can You Be?)

from *Swedish Schnapps +* (Verve 849 393-2)

By Jimmy Davis, Roger Ramirez and Jimmy Sherman

E♭ Alto Saxophone

A Night in Tunisia

from *The Legendary Dial Masters, Vol. I* (Stash ST-CD-23)

By John "Dizzy" Gillespie and Frank Paparelli

Eb Alto Saxophone

Bright Swing ♩ = 180

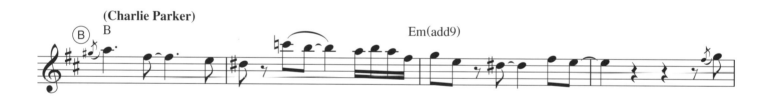

(Charlie Parker)

("Famous" alto break)

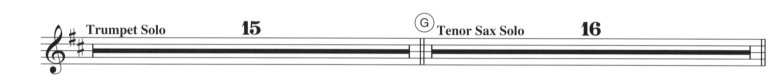

Melody (Miles Davis)

Quasimodo

from *The Legendary Dial Masters, Vol. I* (Stash ST-CD-23)

By Charlie Parker

Ornithology

from *The Legendary Dial Masters, Vol. I* (Stash ST-CD-23)

By Charlie Parker and Bennie Harris

* Bird plays turn on 1st half of out-chorus only.

Relaxin' at Camarillo

from *The Legendary Dial Masters, Vol. I* (Stash ST-CD-23)

By Charlie Parker

Salt Peanuts

from *Dizzy Gillespie-Shaw 'Nuff* (Musicraft MVSCD-53)

By John "Dizzy" Gillespie and Kenny Clarke

Eb Alto Saxophone

Salt pea-nuts, salt pea-nuts.

Star Eyes

from *Swedish Schnapps +* (Verve 849 393-2)

Words and Music by Don Raye and Gene De Paul

The Song Is You

from *Now's the Time* (Verve 825 671-2)

Lyrics by Oscar Hammerstein II
Music by Jerome Kern

Eb Alto Saxophone

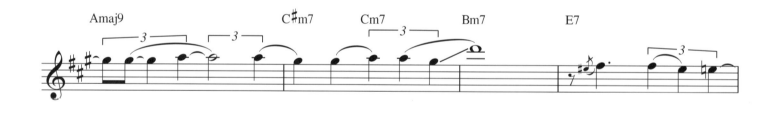

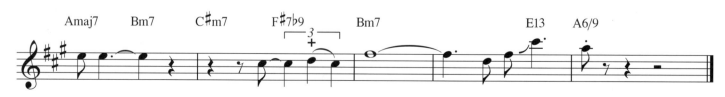